For my favourite Egyptologists,
Nina and Marie.

– T.F.

First published 2021 by Nosy Crow Ltd
The Crow's Nest, 14 Baden Place,
Crosby Row, London SE1 1YW
www.nosycrow.com

ISBN 978 1 78800 901 0

Nosy Crow and associated logos are trademarks
and/or registered trademarks of Nosy Crow Ltd.

Published in collaboration with the British Museum.
With special thanks to Marie Vandenbeusch and John Taylor
at the British Museum for their contribution and advice.

Text © Nosy Crow 2021
Illustrations © Tom Froese 2021

A CIP catalogue record for this book is available from the British Library.

Printed in China.
Papers used by Nosy Crow are made from wood
grown in sustainable forests.

1 3 5 7 9 8 6 4 2

Mummies Unwrapped
Contents

What is a mummy?

Over 5,000 years ago, a famous ancient civilisation of pharaohs began in Egypt, North Africa. They believed in life after death and thought that if their dead bodies were preserved, or looked after, their spirits would live forever in an afterlife. We call these preserved human bodies . . . mummies!

The word 'mummy' comes from the Persian word *mumiya*, which means 'bitumen' – a black, sticky, tar-like liquid. When preserved bodies were first discovered hundreds of years ago, they often looked as if they were covered in bitumen, so they became known as mummies. Nowadays, the whole process of preserving a body is known as mummification, or embalming.

The ancient Egyptians believed that every person had three spirits which survived after death:

THE KA
The person's life energy

THE BA
The person's personality

THE AKH
The person's soul

It was very important for Egyptians to protect the dead body because these spirits lived inside it. They believed the spirits would need to recognise the body after death so that they could live forever.

How exactly were mummies made?

Ordinary Egyptians could have their bodies mummified, but it was a very complicated and expensive process. Only the rich and the royal could afford the best materials.

Dead bodies start to rot very quickly – especially in the hot sun – so embalmers had to start making the mummy as soon as possible. It took a whole team of embalmers a very long time!

First, they would collect the dead body and take it to a 'tent of purification' known as an ibu. This was a tent made from reeds and mats and it was usually close to the River Nile so they could use fresh water. Here, the embalmers would get rid of any liquid left in the body, like blood, before washing it in water and natron (a kind of salt).

After the body had been cleaned, it was taken to an embalmer's workshop, known as a wabet.

Meet the embalmers:

The MASTER OF SECRETS was in charge. Some people believe that he wore the mask of the god Anubis, who was the first to perform mummification.

An embalmer's toolkit:

A SPECIAL FLINT KNIFE
To cut the body open

A FUNNEL
For injecting resin into the skull through the nostrils

PALM WINE
To clean the body after the organs were removed

LINEN
To make the bandages

NATRON
A natural salt that soaks up moisture and breaks down fat

RESIN
To cover the body once it had been stuffed

PERFUME AND OILS
To make the skin smell sweeter

SAWDUST, SAND AND MUD
To stuff the body

The SLICER cut down the line and removed the internal organs. As soon as he cut the body, he would run away from the workshop, with other people chasing after him throwing stones.

The PRIEST read out sacred texts and spells.

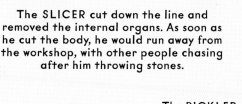

The SCRIBE drew a line down the left-hand side of the stomach.

The PICKLER preserved the organs.

What happened to the organs?

The Egyptians believed it was important to look after the internal organs. They took great care to leave the heart in place because it would be needed again in the afterlife.

The rest of the main organs were removed through a cut in the stomach and stored in canopic jars. An embalmer would usually reach a hand inside the body and pull the organs out!

The STOMACH was stored in a jar with the head of DUAMUTEF, the jackal.

The INTESTINES were stored in a jar with the head of QEBEHSENUEF, the falcon.

The LUNGS were stored in a jar with the head of HAPI, the baboon.

The LIVER was stored in a jar with the head of IMSETY, the human.

Canopic jars came in all kinds of designs and were made from different materials. Usually each jar had a lid that looked like the head of one of the four Sons of Horus, an important god in Egypt.

To stop the organs rotting, they would be soaked in natron. Once there was no moisture left, they were coated in resin, wrapped in linen and placed inside a canopic jar with the lid screwed tightly.

The jars were then stored inside a canopic chest, which was placed inside the tomb next to the mummy. For the rich and royal, each bundle of organs could be placed inside its own coffin – just like mini mummies!

The Egyptians didn't take care of all the organs though . . . in fact, they destroyed the brain! To protect the shape of the head itself, embalmers used a long iron hook to reach up through the nose, mash up the brain and pull it out through the nostril in small pieces. Sometimes they would take the brain out through the back of the head instead.

Cheaper mummies could be made by injecting cedar oil into the body. This turned the insides to liquid, which drained out the bottom!

The empty body was washed out with palm wine and spices. This part of making a mummy usually happened very quickly, but the next stage took a lot longer . . .

How did they rebuild the mummy?

It was now time to dry out the body completely. It was covered in heaps of natron, which was also packed inside the body in tiny linen packages.

After around 35 days, the skin would be hard and wrinkled – it looked like leather stretched tight over the skeleton – and the body would be half the weight it was before.

The next stage was transforming the mummy into something as lifelike and beautiful as possible.

Beeswax and animal fats were poured into the body and over the skin to soften it. To make the mummy smell nicer, embalmers massaged the skin with scented oils, like frankincense and myrrh.

They wanted to make the mummy smell like a god.

Then the embalmers stuffed the body with rolls of linen, sawdust, mud and dried plants. To plump up any shrivelled bits, they pushed stuffing into tiny cuts and smoothed out the surface. They took special care to stuff the face, but sometimes the cheeks were stuffed so much, they actually burst open!

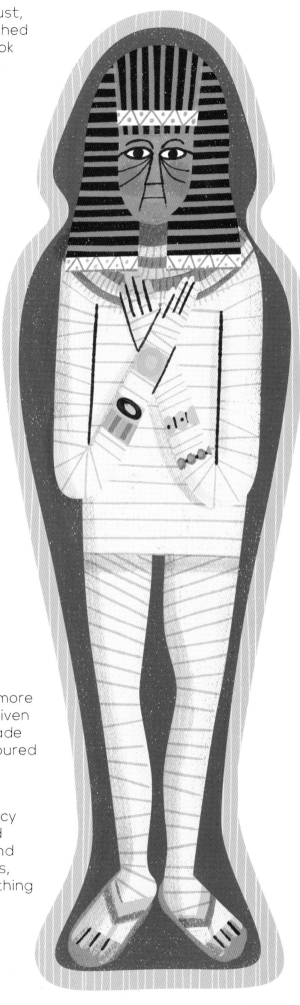

Mummy Mistakes!

Mummy-making didn't always go to plan. If body parts were missing – either through injury or disease, or during the process – some embalmers made fake body parts out of wood or linen instead!

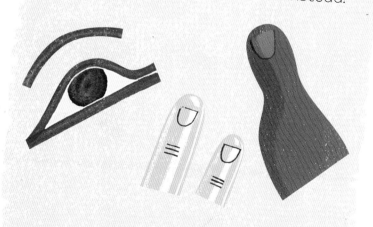

To make the mummy look more alive, it was given false eyes made of stone, coloured glass or even onions!

The most fancy mummies had gold finger and toe caps, wigs, make-up, clothing and jewellery.

How were mummies wrapped?

Once the mummy looked as good as possible, the body was wrapped. This protected the body in its journey to the afterlife – both physically and spiritually. During the wrapping, a priest read out special spells to add an extra layer of protection.

The wrappings were usually made of linen. For important mummies they used cloth which had been used in religious ceremonies, but poorer people used old cloth like bedsheets! The material was torn into long thin strips that looked like bandages.

The most common wrapping technique was to start by wrapping the head, then the arms and legs separately, then the whole body.

Mummy Mistakes!

Some mummies were wrapped the wrong way around or ended up lying face-down or with a mask on their feet. Once, a mummy was found that contained tiny mice and lizards that had got stuck between the wrappings!

Linen was soaked in oil or resin to glue the bandages together and linen pads were placed in between the layers to give the mummy a more rounded shape. Mummies were wrapped in about 20 layers, so they needed to be lifted up and turned over a lot. The most complicated mummies could take up to 30 days to complete!

Once the mummy was completely covered in strips, it was wrapped in a large rectangular sheet, called a shroud, which was tied in place with more linen. Some mummies ended up wrapped in 375 metres of linen . . .

. . . that's enough to stretch along almost 4 football pitches!

How were mummies buried?

Now, the mummy needed a few final touches. It wasn't complete until it had a mask, of course! This was so the person could be recognised in the afterlife, but the face didn't always look very realistic. It was painted to look young, fresh and beautiful.

Masks were usually made from cartonnage – layers of linen soaked in glue and plaster. It was just like papier-mâché so it could be easily shaped when wet and painted when dry. Some masks were made from gold, covered in a fine gold leaf or painted yellow to look like gold.

Golden jewellery was added to the mummy to show how rich the person was and small charms called amulets were tucked inside the wrappings to provide even more magical protection.

SCARAB
To protect the heart

HEADREST
To keep the head with the body

TYET
Isis, to protect the neck

DJED PILLAR
Osiris, a symbol of stability

SHEN
Represents eternity

PAPYRUS COLUMN
To keep the limbs strong

FALCON
Represents Horus

WEDJAT
Eye of Horus, a healing symbol

Egyptians believed that the container they were buried in was important too. Poor people would have a plain wooden box, but very rich Egyptians would have a number of human-shaped coffins that would fit inside each other and the inner one could sometimes even be solid gold!

Coffins came in all shapes and sizes, but most were decorated with special spells and pictures that Egyptians believed would help them in the afterlife.

What happened at a funeral?

After 70 days, the mummy was finally ready to be buried and there was a funeral procession to take the body to the tomb. This was a resting place for the mummy and somewhere people could visit to leave messages from the world of the living.

Poor people were buried in simple graves in the desert, but tombs for the royals needed to last forever, so they were made from stone. The giant pyramids were actually built as a tomb for just one king!

At a funeral procession, the coffin was placed on a boat and dragged along on a sledge. Priests would lead the way to the tomb, burning sweet-smelling incense and reciting spells. A group of female mourners would walk behind the coffin, singing sad songs, wailing loudly and beating their hands against their bodies to show how upset they were.

Servants would carry all the things they believed the dead person would need in the afterlife – furniture, clothing, jewellery, musical instruments, even chariots! These were called grave goods. Rich Egyptians even took little mummy-shaped figures called shabtis, which could act as servants.

Once the procession reached the tomb the mummy was stood upright and a priest performed a special ceremony called 'Opening of the Mouth'.

Here, the priest would use a sacred tool to touch the mouth on the mummy's mask. This would wake up its senses, so the mummy could breathe, see, hear, speak and taste again. Then, the coffin was taken inside the pyramid or tomb and put inside an outer stone coffin called a sarcophagus. It usually had a pair of eyes painted or carved on the side, so the mummy could see their way to the afterlife.

What happened to the mummies next?

Many tombs were made up of two parts – a burial chamber for the mummy and a place for people to leave their offerings. It was the duty of the family to bring food and drink to the tomb forever so the mummy's spirit could live on, but, if this didn't happen, the walls of the tomb were painted with magical spells to help.

On the way to the afterlife, the mummy had to pass a 'Weighing of the Heart' ceremony. They believed Anubis, the jackal-headed god, would weigh the heart of their soul against the 'feather of truth'. If the heart was heavier, it would be eaten by a hippopotamus-lion-crocodile creature, but if the heart was lighter, they could continue on their journey.

Once the mummy was inside the tomb, the burial chamber was meant to stay sealed for ever, but that wasn't always the case . . .

Tombs were often a target for thieves because mummies were buried with such valuable objects. Even linen and glass could be stolen and sold for a lot of money.

Robbers would secretly tunnel through the stone, burn down the coffins and rip open the mummies' wrappings to get to the treasure hidden inside.

21

What about animal mummies?

Animals were used for hunting, they were pets, they were eaten as food and they were also thought of as messengers of the gods, so why were they turned into mummies too?

Pets were sometimes mummified at the same time as their humans, so they could stay together in the afterlife. Dogs, cats, gazelles, monkeys – each animal was carefully embalmed and given its own little wooden coffin, whether it was ready to go or not!

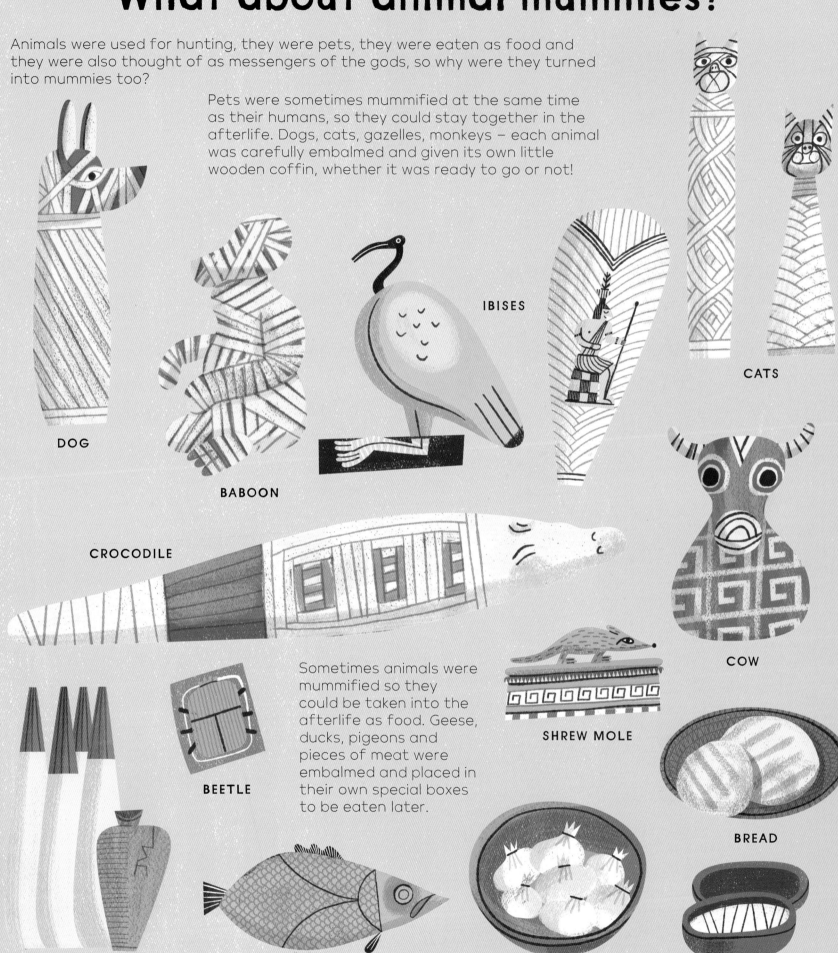

DOG

BABOON

IBISES

CATS

CROCODILE

COW

Sometimes animals were mummified so they could be taken into the afterlife as food. Geese, ducks, pigeons and pieces of meat were embalmed and placed in their own special boxes to be eaten later.

SHREW MOLE

BEETLE

BREAD

BEER

FISH

FIGS

MEAT

The ancient Egyptians believed animals represented gods – either as whole animals or as humans with the head of an animal.

Egyptians thought some very powerful animals, like the Apis bull, had special powers so it was treated just like a god. They lived in temples and were looked after by priests and, when the bull died, it was mummified and had a grand funeral procession – just like a king! Some bull mummies have even been discovered with masks and hooves made of solid gold.

Mummified animals were often taken to temples as gifts to honour the gods. This was called a votive offering. Cat mummies were given to the goddess Bastet who was represented by a cat. It was believed that these offerings would bring people closer to the god itself and some tombs had rooms containing millions of mummies!

Mummy Mistakes!

Animal mummies weren't always what they seemed . . . People would sell fake mummies to use as votive offerings. Sometimes the mummies weren't animals at all – just wrapped up sand, mud, sticks, feathers and rags – and sometimes the fakes contained parts of two different animals stuck together!

What happened when mummies were discovered?

Thousands of years after they were buried, people in Europe started to become interested in mummies too.

During the Middle Ages, it was believed the bitumen sometimes used in embalming had magical healing powers. People began digging up mummies, grinding them to a powder and selling it as medicine. The French King Francis I carried a packet of powdered mummy with him at all times in case he ever urgently needed healing!

By the 1500s, so much mummy powder was being sent to Europe, Egypt started to create fake mummies using recent dead bodies.

However, by the 1800s, people had started to realise that mummies didn't make the best medicine after all . . .

Instead, it became fashionable among rich Europeans to travel to Egypt and bring ancient mummies home as souvenirs! Back in England, the Victorians would sell tickets to 'mummy unwrapping' parties, where audiences were mostly interested in the mysterious, magical amulets.

We know so much about mummies today because they haven't stayed underground forever. But nowadays, if a new mummy is found, it is very rarely unwrapped. Instead, experts use technology like X-rays and CAT scans to learn about mummies without destroying them.

Occasionally, fake mummies turned out not to be ancient at all! During this time, mummies were also used as:

PAPER
It was reported that linen mummy wrappings were used by a butcher in the US to wrap up his meat – until he was blamed for an outbreak of cholera.

FERTILISER
A huge number of cat mummies were shipped to England, where they were ground up to be used as plant fertiliser.

PAINT
Ground-up mummy remains were used to create an oil paint called Mummy Brown. Paint companies were still making it until the 1960s!

FIREWOOD
Mummies were often used as fuel for fires and tomb robbers had been known to rip off a mummy's arm or leg to light as a torch.

Who are some of the most famous mummies?

In the late 1800s, people started to believe spooky stories about ancient mummies coming back to life. Then, in 1922, archaeologist Howard Carter discovered a royal tomb that had never been explored before. It was still sealed, so nobody knew what lay inside!

Years later, Carter and his team finally reached the burial chamber . . . There, they found the mummy of King Tutankhamun, a young pharaoh who had ruled Egypt thousands of years ago. The mummy itself wasn't in good condition, but Tutankhamun's tomb was full of some of the greatest treasure ever found.

A rich aristocrat that had helped Carter, Lord Carnarvon, died from an infected mosquito bite soon after the tomb was opened, which led people to believe that the mummy really was cursed after all . . .

The mummy of Tutankhamun may be the most famous, but he's not the only one to have an interesting story. Here are just a few of the many well-known Egyptian mummies that are on display in museums around the world:

SETY I

The mummy of pharaoh Sety I had been taken out of his elaborate tomb and hidden to protect his remains. When he was eventually discovered, his body had been badly damaged by tomb robbers, but his face remained untouched.

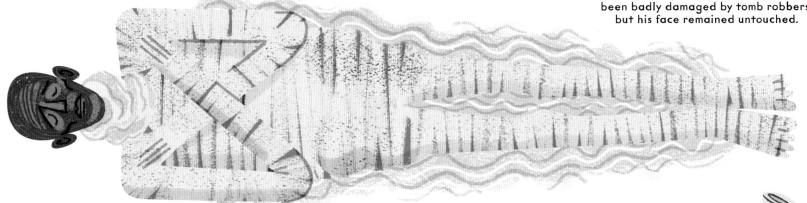

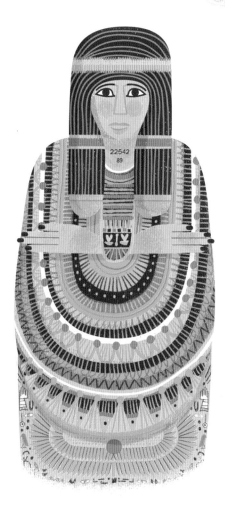

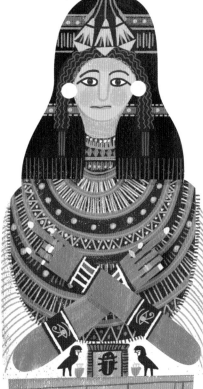

MAN FROM GEBELEIN

One of the earliest Egyptian mummies was a man from Gebelein, who had striking ginger hair. He died around 3400 BC, before the Egyptians had started mummifying the dead, and his body was dried naturally in the hot sand.

THE UNLUCKY MUMMY

The 'unlucky mummy' is not actually a mummy at all. In fact, it's a painted board that was supposed to be placed on top of a real mummy. It's said to have been cursed, bringing bad luck on its owners, with some people believing it sank on the *Titanic*!

KATEBET

Katebet had been very carefully wrapped on the outside, but inside her body was packed with lots of mud!

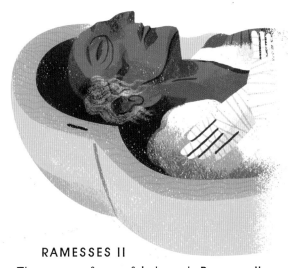

RAMESSES II

The mummy of powerful pharaoh, Ramesses II, was discovered in 1881 in the same secret royal tomb as Sety I. Almost a century later, archaeologists noticed the mummy was in very bad condition so flew him to Paris for special treatment. He was issued an Egyptian passport before the journey, where he was described as 'King (deceased).'

Glossary

AFTERLIFE – Beginning a new life after death

AMULET – A small piece of jewellery or object thought to give protection against danger or evil

ARCHAEOLOGIST – Someone who studies history by digging up and examining historical objects

CANOPIC JARS – Four special jars used to store a mummified person's liver, lungs, intestines and stomach that were buried alongside the mummy

CARTONNAGE – A material made from layers of linen soaked in glue and plaster

CAT SCAN – A kind of X-ray that can show very detailed pictures of the inside of an object or person

CHARIOT – An ancient two-wheeled vehicle that was pulled by horses

CHOLERA – A disease of the small intestine

CIVILISATION – A large, well-organised group of people that live together with their own language and way of life

COFFIN – A box to hold a dead body

EMBALMING – Using salt or other chemicals to stop a body from rotting

ETERNITY – Lasting forever

FERTILISER – A substance that is added to the soil to help plants to grow

FLINT – A very hard stone

IBU – A special 'tent of purification' where the dead body was cleaned

INCENSE – A material that is burned to produce a nice smell

LINEN – A light, cool fabric made from the flax plant

MIDDLE AGES – A period in European history between ancient and modern times, between AD 500 and 1500

MOURNER – Someone who attends the funeral of a friend or relative

MUMMIFICATION – An ancient Egyptian method of preserving a dead body by turning the person into a mummy

NATRON – A type of salt used to dry dead bodies as part of the embalming or mummification process

OFFERING – Something given to the gods

ORGAN – A part of the human body that has job to do

PERSIAN – A language spoken in Persia, which is modern-day Iran

PHARAOH – A king or ruler

PYRAMID – A large stone tomb built for a pharaoh

RESIN – A thick liquid that comes from trees

RIVER NILE – The longest river in the world

SACRED – Special or holy

SARCOPHAGUS – Stone coffin

SERVANT – Somebody who works in somebody else's home

SHABTI – A small human-shaped figure that represented servants

TEMPLE – A building for religious ceremonies and worship of the gods

TOMB – A place for burying a dead person, either underground or in a special building

WABET – An embalmer's workshop

X-RAY – Powerful waves of energy that can show pictures of the inside of an object or person

Index

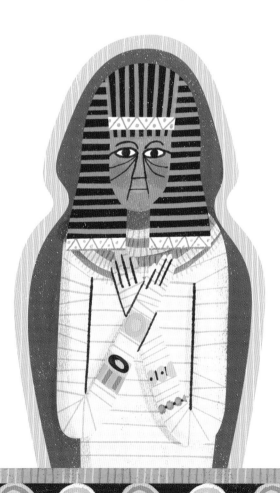

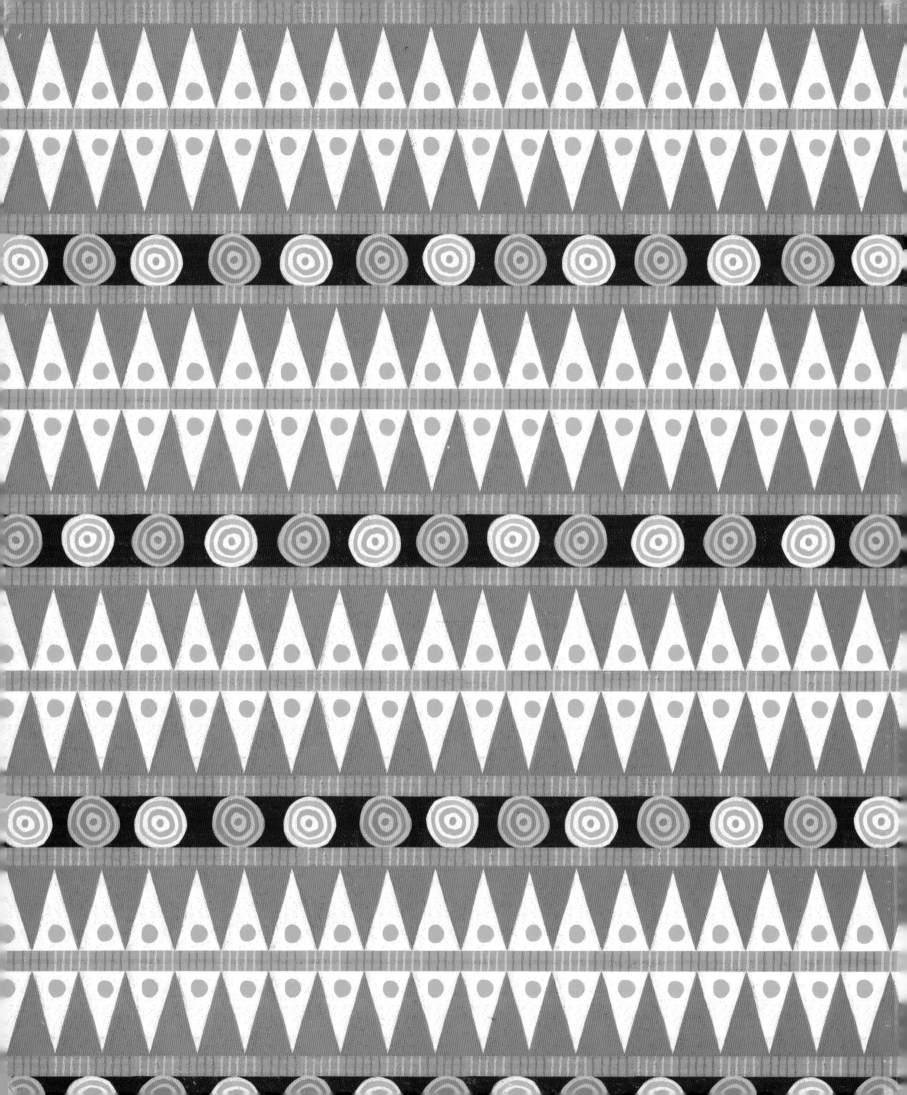